potbellied stove
and other poems by
george d. clabon

cover, art and book design
by Ginny Knight

International Standard Book Number 1-890459-00-3
Library Of Congress Catalog Card Number 97-60486
Copyright © 1997 TA Publications

ALL RIGHTS RESERVED
Reproduction in whole or in part without written permission is prohibited,
except by a reviewer who may quote brief passages in a review.

Printed in the United States of America

*to my mother
Lillie A. Clabon
with love*

contents

potbellied stove 1
when freedom came 2
in the city 3
the legend of sleepy pat 3
mr. thom and sleepy pat 4
the bear 6
ghost riders 7
the junkman (role model 2) 7
recipe for a live young one 8
cross jefferson 9
cork 10
childish game 11
the creeps 12
teacher's strike 13
words of women 14
manly 15
a thousand hells 15
better housing 16
the hourglass 18
value added (wearing bally's) 18
healing herbs 19
home 19
somewhere tonight 20
job descripton (our house) 20
community involvement 21
gaining surface 22
weapons of dishonor 23
welcome 24
for e. smalley 25
talking to dolores 26
chasing the ball 26
the merger 27

where dennis sang	28
basketball junkies	29
renewal of spirits	30
home run	31
much like dennis	32
abc-priority ranking	33
OJT	33
seeking success	34
appropriate attire	35
(job) pride	36
product harvesting	38
truthfully speaking	39
shrimp boil	39
struggling economics	40
stephen's tale	41
talking about (signs of hope)	42
the value of waiting	42
out of the chasm	43
on this night	44
swimming lessons	45
graveyard love	46
fade away	46
eternal togetherness (keys please)	47
shared lust	48
getting some	48
weighing possibilities	49
please, leave a message	49
deeper, i fall	50
soul to soul	50
curtain call	51
images of love	52
freedom	52
in the background	53
the verdict	54
you be to me	54
planting the seed	55
morning thoughts	55
dreams	56
the wanderer	56
slow slide	57
looking at you	57
double dipping	58
scorpio's ascendency	58
better day	59
all	59
a new meaning	60

potbellied stove

i watch the fire
    through the grill
        of the potbellied stove
as it heats
    our house
        (sitting in her chair
            she watches over us
            as she prays . . .

    the strong woman

        that's what i need
        to be, lord

    the strong woman

        to take care
        of these children
        you've blessed me with

    the strong woman

        to walk this path

            lord

        i need you with me
            my children
            need you

        to walk this path

        i need to be
            strong

        in you, lord
            for without you

        i am alone
            as my children

        who need you)

i watch the fire
    of the strong woman

when freedom came

      it's said
that harry keogh
      has the gift

to converse with the dead

      so i called him
to converse with my great
      ancestor

(i don't know why
      my mistress
decided to hide me
under the wash tub

from the union soldiers

      as they proceeded
to march my brothers
      back to bondage

for they had not taken
      up arms
they were not included

when freedom came)

in the city

      we walked into the restroom
in the Port Authority's basement
after parking Cliff's Regal
and stepped over the homeless
lying barefoot on the floor
      to use the urinals

how came this man to be like this
      i know not
in a land of dreams
so like thousand of others
i turned and walked away
caring not
      while longing to care
how this man came to be like this

in the city . . .

the legend of sleepy pat

here i was
    steppin' off the edge
of the plane
    into no where

      i'd ever been
      before

monroe, louisiana
    what was this place
    where i'd come
to hear the stories
    of sleepy pat

      as best
      aunt big gal
      could recall

mr. thom and sleepy pat
(conversation with the necroscope)

harry
>*i know you got to go*
>>*soon*

for the bloodsuckers scourge
>*be upon us*
>>*you our hope*

>>>*stay a while*
>>>>*longer*
>>*so we may talk to our descendant*

   i met sleepy pat
   not a bad fellow
   though he not from
   oak grove

   you know he used to say
   "no 'bacca, no work"

   don't get me wrong
   he was a hard worker
      but
   "no 'bacca, no work"

   although he'd blame it
      on his mule
   say that the only way
      that mule
   would pull the plow

      yep,
   that sleepy pat
      he alright

   although i think
      he stole my line

   you know,
      all shut eyes
      ain't sleep

mr. thom
    you think
        you the only one
    with words
        before harry goes?

i know i don't say much
    that's the way we be
        down gilbert way

    say lot
without saying lot

        next to fishing
    not more to learn

the bloodsuckers scourge
    is upon us
        harry
    you must go

do come visit again
so we may talk to
    our descendant

    remember
all shut eyes
    ain't sleep

the bear

bud stopped
      the bear stood
in the middle of the road
and didn't particularly
      look like moving

bud weighed
      his options
            none too good
no where to run
no where to hide
in the middle of the road

slowly bud
      pulled his knife
      from its sheath
      as the bear rose
to embrace him

in the middle of the road

ghost riders

i seen dem ghost men
dey rode up to de house
tooks my pappy away
we boys were held back
tol' stop cryin'
'cause ghost men
can take us'n too
if dey want

i stand beneath the oak
it's graceful strength
fading from years of enduring
man's way
i still see the swaying body
from long ago
of the midnight ride
of the ghost men

the junkman (role model 2)

    a wooden cart
was his work tool

mobile by wooden wheels
    similar to those
that fared wagons
    across the plains

    fared him
across jefferson

to the junkyard
    to trade his collections
        for meager coinage

he admonished us children

    not to live
        like him

recipe for a live young one

the perceptive children
watched as Grams kept trying
mixture after mixture
without success
    so they inquired
"What you making, Grandma?"

she responded —
    "It was suggested
    that I obtain this secret recipe
    from the 'Guru of Live Ones'
    by meeting her price:

    a dozen times a dozen
    soda pop cans
    and that many more
    of pull tops from cans
    and the recipe of your desire
    will be yours"

looking at each other in confusion
the grandchildren shrugged
and said . . .
    "Wouldn't it be simpler
    to catch a live young one
    at a garage sale?"

and they returned to their play
as Grams went back to work
    on the perfect recipe
    for a live young one

cross jefferson

we boys sat
    beneath the porch
in the cool
    coming from

the basement

talking 'bout waking
      'bout walking
   in spirit

(23rd psalms

says it every morning
just like mama taught us

   says it

when i go
cross jefferson

they don't like us
alley boys

cross jefferson)

we boys sat . . .

cork

the rules of the game
were simple enough
    if only three played
        you took a chance
        at each position
batter/pitcher/catcher

the one I dreaded most
watching that broomstick
swing in front of my eyes
    as I attempted to field
    their imitation of Bob

and if you knocked it
onto Jefferson
that was automatic
    out that is
for 'twas unnecessary
    dangerous
    and costly
for we wouldn't pay
for broken windshields
for balls we hit not
    for we be broke too

and any ball
hit past the pitcher
    be fly or ground
advanced the runner
to the appropriate bag
those in front of the hurler
would have been a sure out
for the infield
    and, oh yeah
        one strike, you out
        two fouls, you out
keeps the game moving
keeps the young minds interested
keeps them off the streets
and on Kroger's lot
under watchful eyes

       cork
the game of my youth
     is stick ball
      really similar
consider it
as changing winds blow

childish game

it's just a game
    just a childish game
we'd sometimes play

   give me
           4-teen words
           outta *'bottom'*
    not using
prepositions
proper names
         in say
   3 minutes

bet u can't do it
   my bogie says
   u can't

just a game
    just a childish game . . .

the creeps

i feel them
    stepping out of the shadows
from around the corner
    of my storage bin

    creeping up on me

    (I really could use
      That dollar
        Gene offered

    Take his Bannisters

      Let me correct my self
    Bannister Alligators

      To the shine parlor
    On Easton
      If that shop closed
        Go to the one
    On Franklin

    My palms began to sweat
      Anticipation of the payment

    For the shop on Easton
      Be closed on Sundays
    So I tightened my grip
      On my pocket knife

    My family could use
      That dollar

    As I handed
      The Bannister Alligators
    To the creepers
      On Franklin

    But not the visage
      Of George
    For my family)

i feel them creeping
    up on me
        this night . . .

teacher's strike

sitting at the cafeteria table
my meager lunch in front of me
    hamburger made from soybean extract
    mashed potatoes by Uncle Ben's
    Campbell's tomato soup
thinking about the good old days
when Dad was in school
    real meat was used instead of synthetics
    fresh vegetables, homemade soup,
        and hot bread
the lunch today reflects the world changes
where only the children shall suffer

sitting at home watching T.V.
i wish i was in my home room
    studying English, Calculus, or Physics
    instead of wasting my mind
while the teachers stay out for better pay
unlike the good old days
    mom studied Economics and History
    dad studied Agriculture
teachers had pets and taught school
    greed was not their motive
which reflects the times of today
were only the children shall suffer

words of women
(*right* of passage)

     maybe
you should not hunt
    today
there is plenty
         in the store room

he looked at her
as his companions waited
for the male bonding
of the hunt

for his last outing

as he listened not
to the words
of his woman
it wasn't like her dream
foretold the future

    at least
leave the boy behind
    from today's
right of passage

as they pulled off
he wondered
should he have left the boy

(somewhere tonight . . .)

manly

i cry
      in the dark

(i looked at them
      models

displaying emotions
      manly

at the graveside

though each loved
      the same as those

that were not
      manly)

in the dark
      i cry . . .

a thousand hells

into the night
of a thousand hells
      i walk

a releasing of the inner self
with what we call the intoxicants
      of our choice
realizing not
the destruction of inner self

      i walk blindly
into the thousand hells
at night

better housing

as Donnie sang
about the Ghetto
and lessons learned
    therein

we missed it
dealing with survival . . .

i looked up
at the newly constructed
buildings of the future
from beneath the billboard
that occupied the lot
next to the first house
of the block
    and wondered
what occupancy was like

they had little lawns
enclosed by chain link fences
    (as down the generations
    they haunt my people
        shackles)
big enough
for maybe three kids
    not enough room
    for a good marbles contest
and lots of concrete
    easy
    to bruise/batter/break
    an opponent
    in a fight
        or be the recipient
        of same

but the attraction
most of all
was the absence from view
of any cooling units
    as everyone knows
    hot/humid/heat
    rises
ventilation was provided
by windows on one side

i understood
the tenants frustration
    of a request not met
    for better housing
and wished not
to reside in one
    (little did we know
    they were the first
    condos)

as Donnie sang
about the Ghetto . . .

the hourglass

the sands of time
fall within the hourglass
while we react as though
they stand still

due to a halloween party
he walks with the ancestors
as does she
that turned her back
on the provisions provider

did the founders envision
that bearing of arms
would be required
beyond their time

the sands of time
fall within the hourglass . . .

value added (wearing bally's)

shoes, shoes
      for sale

not in my hood
      cause we bring

      value down

      or so it's said

like when we move
      into your hood

shoes, shoes
      for sale . . .

healing herbs

no longer fit the bill
to providing good health

thousands still wait
for the trickle down

home

the demons of destruction
ride the elevators at Chase House

ripping the padding off the walls
tossing empty beer cans in the corner

knocking out panels in the ceiling
pushing the buttons to every floor

writing graphic obscenities
fueling their perverse humor

another eight percent
added to the monthly rent
      when the lease expires

for the cleaning lady in the halls
picking up after the wild bunch

the replacing of carpets and lights
by the maintenance crew

at the place they call home

somewhere tonight

a mother cries
for her child
has passed on

she beseeches
the wisdom giver
to show her
why
her child
had to leave
now

she cries out
in her anguish
at receiving not
the wisdom

somewhere tonight

job description (our house)

you   big man
        dominate inside
defensively   offensively

let them know
    you   big man

gots to pay
    come to our house

shot block / hard foul / hard pick

cause
    you   big man

without you   we have
    no house

community involvement

back before the emergence
of the new ideology
    i got mine
    you deal with your'n
our inhabitants
were community involved
    like Willie Jr. . . .

    as I entered puberty
when others in my stage
of development
    bought suits of brown
    to earn badges of honor
and those in my sector
    of economics
felt excluded from organizations
aimed at youth enrichment

    he brought us together
    as a group
where we grew to understand
that the only unconquerable barriers
    are mental
    not materialistic

    there once was honor
and a sense of pride
in helping the children
of your neighborhood grow
    but that was before
the emergence of the new ideology
    i got
    mine . . .

gaining surface

the under current
    pulls me lower
        as i struggle
to gain the surface
to gain the meaning

    of family

i walked
into the rehab center
looked around
    with confusion
at those absent
and dealt with
the meaning

    of family

and my contribution
to the meaning

as i extended
my arms
to those absent
embracing them
into my meaning

    of family

i gained the surface

weapons of dishonor

a being
      passed on today

      matters not
      if i approved
           of the lifestyle
           of the being
who passed on today

(marco, marco, marco
you lied to us
promised not to
      dishonor   us
by building weapons
      of destruction
      of dishonor

when we showed you
fireworks making

we've been joined
by the fruit
of your deceit

as our numbers   grow
from your use
      of fireworks making)

today a being
      passed on

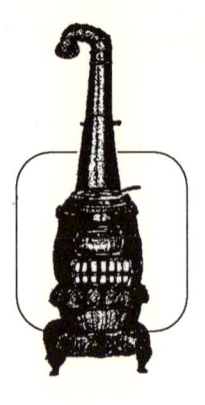

welcome

   a child
born innoncently into this world
to fulfill the dream
   of a parent

to cherish and nourish with love
and understanding
   to bring new light
into a family's heart
   with its smile

for this life, Father
thanks is given to thee
and we ask that you bestow
your blessings on this child

we, your family and friends
bid thee welcome
   child

for e. smalley

      as he drove off
in his powder blue '54 olds
after a rousing round of b-ball
with the fellas
      our sunday morning ritual
at the park of the commoners

      i thought of the road
      he had travelled
he passed a lot of construction
as he donned out on the trip
of single parenthood
      his son and daughter
      snuggled in the back seat
            with not a worry
      cause dad was at the wheel

      so he proceeded with care
made sure they did not jostle
      when he hit bumps
      along the way
because their safety and welfare
came first in his mind
      he would ensure
they reached their destination
unscathed

      i feel proud
      to call him friend

talking to dolores

when we converse
    i feel the lesson
    she learned

at her grandpa's feet

    (now, you take du'bois
        and his talented tenth

    he talking about knowledge
        being passed on
    to those that want knowledge

    he right
cause you can't make one
    take knowledge

    so baby girl
you want to teach
    when you grow up)

chasing the ball

    we
are but shadows
of our former selves

    as
we chase the ball
of our youth

    with
fond remembrance
of past glory

    of
chasing the ball
in our youth

the merger
(legend of phynque inc.)

shortly after i began my stint
at the rock
brad called me into his office
laid his cards on the table

he spread hill, suggs, webster
an o.b. and a miller
plus himself, brad the coach

i spread homeboys from the 'field
doughboy, jones, lil' mike
a foreman and travis
plus me, big g

we merged our hands
to take the floor at golden valley
starting the hoops legend
of phynque inc.

where dennis sang

there was dennis
reminding me of dennis

(hold up
      wait a minute
where you goin' now?)

rodman - spears
      both brothers
demonstrate their talents
      on the court
      of their blessing

(oh,   had to check
'cause i thought
      you meant
      the menace
      named dennis
was back!)

naw,   i'm talking 'bout
      bill and jerry's
      where dennis sang

basketball junkies

march madness
                yes!!!

my time of year
as college ball
advances towards
                accolades
of being the best
while the pros
become serious
about playoffs

what more
could a junkie
ask for?

(what's that you say?
a city/state
            championship?

how old are you?
have you truly
              gone mad
with this march
              madness?
best to turn the tube
            off)

huh!
what did you say
              dear?

oh yeah,
        got the fellas
coming by
for march madness
        okay?

cause you know
        we basketball
                junkies!!!

(the boy's
        truly mad)

renewal of spirits
(times of bonding)

whenever i felt
          my spirit
begin that long slow
          walk
down the road of self/
      pity/self
          doubt
due to being with
      self/alone

i'd trip on over
to the house
for a spiritual
      uplifting

a renewal of self

(Michael and Bruce
          Did the D'Artagnan
Warren, Kirk, Ernest
and my man from around the way
Corn-Dex
      Did the Chi step
While Mildred and I
      Did the St. Louis bop
As we partied in "The House"
During the times
      Of Bonding)

i feel my spirit
      in need of
renewal

(Mattie and Kevin and Erich
Cry out
      Party over here
Arnold and Hazel and Geno
Respond
      Party over where!

And we say
      Party everywhere
At "The House")

home run

after the softball game
we stood around
finishing the Old Milwaukee
    rehashing the plays

if only the left center
had caught that last fly
    instead of losing it in the sun
we would have won

as another bottle was passed
a cycle spewed gravel
    into the air
the bike slid along the road
    from under the rider
    as he left the playing field
we found humor
in his minor bumps and bruises

never considering
what price we pay for fun
    as we prepared
        ourselves
    for the run home

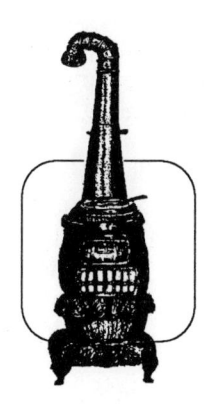

much like dennis
(salary treatment)

i didn't know
    i still had the lift
in these legs

i contemplated
        as i rebounded
        the missed shot
and rose to return it
    scoring the attempt
    of my teammate

and dennis does this
all the time
where does his stamina
come from
'cause this rebounding
be tiring work
'bout as back breaking
as working the field

(see, see
there you go again
comparing sports men
to field hands

you ain't right
'cause field hands
didn't get the same
salary treatment)

i turn to follow
    my teammates
in hopes of garnering
    another rebound
to assist
    in another basket

much like dennis

abc-priority ranking
(placing of friendship)

i watch

    as you change
    from casual conversation
    in the shared setting
to negotiation
    of time
      with significant other
    on the phone

and i'm able

    to place
my priority ranking
    within
      your life

OJT
(on the job training)

in a classroom of thirty we sat
listening to the creak of the chairs
people shifting nervously about

water on each table for those dry throats
ashtrays for those smoked filled lungs
the speaker cleared his throat for attention

anxiously we all awaited his words of wisdom
feeling special to be the ones chosen
no attention was paid to our surroundings

the smell of brimstone was sweet to us
we watched the fire as the speaker said
"my name is Dante and I bid thee welcome"

seeking success

huffing and puffing
i gain the last
few steps
to your perch

the knowledgeable one
providing answers
to those who seek
to inquire

to those who seek
to travel

for 'tain't easy
getting to your perch

i pose my question
of attaining success

(within each
       organization
lies pockets of power
based on likeness

one must understand
how to work with
the pockets

payment please)

i thought how much
you sound like
the good magician
       humphrey

as i pay the price
of seeking...

appropriate attire
(networking)

i push the mail cart
through the various divisions
    talking to the workers
inquiring about their duties
as quickly as possible
    for i follow the rules
        but
it's my net/work outlet
as i'm excluded
    from network venues
because economically
i cannot afford
    the required attire

(what happened to the days
of shirt and tie
acceptability
for upward mobility
expression?

don't tell me
    disruptive forces
okay!!)

as i net/work
    pushing the mail cart
i dream of the day
i can be like
    those
who are attired appropriately
    to network

(job) pride

as I go thru my routine
on a daily basis
supervising a technical section
of insurance specialists
    (or is that overseeing
        oops
           heritage shining thru)

i sometimes miss the positive
for dealing with the negative
of finding loopholes
    to rules
like the lawyer
getting the best deal for his client
    because
that's the bottom line

we have come together
as a unit

we play the numbers game
    become frustrated
because of our inner motivation
to be the best
and achieve the highest grade
in all categories

as we switch channels
like the changing of programs
on the boob tube
    (life is a soap
        ha ha
    this too is heritage
    shining on)

the written communique
received by those on high
give strokes to our motivator

as we strive on
for near excellence

and together as one
we shall rise to the top

the problems and personalities
that cross our desks
sometimes require the patience
associated with saints
    that we claim not to be
so we extend understanding
    (do unto others
        more words of birthright
           nope
    just a simple rule
    with minor exceptions)

the growing of knowledge
    continues
as the apprentices
learn the particulars
of the trade

the teachers of today
shall preserve the future
of tomorrow

product harvesting
(comfort zone)

the prospect
    of starting over

    scares me

i'm familiar with
    the people

that help this product
    bear harvest

that help this product
    to market

i'm comfortable
    working with them

i'm confident
    working beside them

that the harvest
    will be fruitful

starting over
    scares me

for i'm comfortable
    in this culture

truthfully speaking

listening to the voice
speaking on the line

i think of how
i grow weary

of evaluating
their conversation

truthfully speaking

shrimp boil

as i sat down
       replacing the losers
i was informed
       that i would be
            taught
       like the student
    that i be
       how to play
            the game

he did not know
            he was talking to
       a master
       of whistology

i smiled
       as i opened
       the bidding
with a five
       no trump

at the shrimp boil

struggling economics
(early retirement)

as companies continue
                to struggle
within capitalist societal
                  confines

    providing employment
      for all
    on limited budgets

we became defined
              in market strategies
    'cause

trends changes everything
people be unpredictable
crystal balls cannot forecast all
so trend indicators fail

    making them a day late
    in providing employment
      for all

so the early age
              of retirement
              is lowered
              to capture
those whose age group
    i approach

        (but . . .

will option
    be there for me

    as i turn
        in my dreams . . .)

stephen's tale

night
> before the work
>> day

i sign my contract
with self

things to do
> before they come
> like the langoliers

can't escape
> their coming
>> to get you

interruptions

(so why you sign
> the contract?)

like the man said
> things to do
>> before
they come to get
> you

talking about (signs of hope)

i be far removed
> from the streets
>> my feet walked
>>> in youth

to go to the library
cass   downtown

with my fellas
> from gamble street

>> cause they like
>> to read too

so we'd walk together
> while talking about
>> aging

the value of waiting

if you wait
> things will get better
> you'll get what you want
> you'll get wiser
> money will come your way
> you'll get a wife/
>> children/
>>> grandchildren

times will change . . .

you know
> sometimes
>> you can wait too long

out of the chasm

so once again
        i took you within
my chasm

        to consider life
        from another perspective

could you adapt?

        how do you deal
        with concept changes
            real?

can you escape
        the confines

        of your chasm?

on this night

sleep's not forthcoming
      no matter which way
           i turn

it's either my back
      or my dreams

      can't get no rest
           from neither

(I sit across
from the person
I know
wish not to be here

Talking about
our parting paths

So we talk about
mutual interests
of times shared
as we talk about
      good-bye)

sleep's not forthcoming . . .

swimming lessons

i cannot swim
    therefore
i could not reach
    your shore
while still in sight
of the land mass
    we shared

with each passing day
my estimation
of the ship size
needed to reach
    your shore
        changes

as the gap widens
as the sea churns

i regret
my learning not
    to swim

graveyard love

i feel your absence
    as I sit at the table
    sipping Sauvignon Blanc
    awaiting the dinner arrival
i feel the tug
    from beyond the grave
    at the root of my soul
    and know how to escape not
for in my eye
    i see the spectre of your smile
    and hear your voice's laughter
    at my comical remarks
while I'm alone

fade away

    love
when i first saw you
    i knew
    you were the one
but now i'm not so sure

all those things in common
    have faded away
all the faith, trust, hope
    togetherness
    and happiness
until we both feel
    that we too
    must fade away

eternal togetherness (keys, please)

many
        is the night
            i sit at home
        few drinks too many
              and question you
                  on love
between man   and woman

(that's why
        i take the keys, please)

you say
        man meant to be
            like swan
        and mate for life time
            we say
                until
                    court says
                        otherwise

so where be truth
        in your sayings
            or
is it that we misread
        your sayings
                of eternal togetherness

(yo,
    just the keys,
        please)

shared lust

if we wallow
    lustfully
enjoying each moment
    of sharing bodies

what will be
    the commitment
    of consequences

are we willing
    to take responsibility
    of the consequences

are you committed
    to the sharing
    of lust

cause my body
    aches . . .

getting some

    love
a word we use
    to get some

    attention

stroking of self
        esteem

that i'm okay
    wanted by some
        one

    loved by some
        one

that stokes self
        esteem
to give some

attention . . .

weighing possibilities

if i ask you
to dance

would you step
to the flow

would you
access the package
and

decline the offer
to dance

weigh the possibilities
of your response
as i approach

with the offer
to dance

please, leave a message

i love a woman
who loves me
we just can't get together
for you see
this love is a complicated
thing
full of heartbreak
joy and pain

at the beep . . .

deeper, i fall

i cannot stop
    my descent

deeper

into the being
    of you

    i fall

with each word
    we share

i find
    i cannot stop

my descent

soul to soul

in the theater
    i relaxed
    as my arm
    rested on your leg
    'cause

it's all good

my soul settled
    into the moment
    of your reaching
    down to touch
    me

soul to soul

curtain call

there are times in life
that i wish not to play
    on stage

so i enter my sanctuary
and pull the curtain
    on the act

in my times of quiet,
i feel the beat
from my stereo
as i make contact
    with myself

the voices that i hear
give me counsel
to making my dreams
    materialize

these moments i treasure
and share with few,
until the alarm sounds
    for the curtain call
    to reenter the play

images of love

the seer told me
        i still mourn
        your passing

tho' i thought
        i be over that
with the passage of time

(like the painter
i pose my favorite model
in front of me
to create another image
of love)

        the seer
        told me . . .

freedom

i went for a walk
to the gardens
where I had caged the bird

captured her free spirit
to soar the airwaves
that others feared

i took her will to live
my heart saddened
as I opened the cage

giving her wings to float
to the clouds of her dreams
with blessings of my love

as my tears dropped

in the background

monifah croons
        about it being all right

after my week in newark
a break from the regular
                routine
of earning my meager means
        of existence
contributions not appreciated
        in my evaluation

as she sings
        of not having to love
               me

i relate
        the appraisal of service
                given
with words not related
to service   given

and know it's all right
as i plan to move forward
to where service given
        is appreciated

(ah!,
the possibility exists
the boundary of my ego
over estimates
        the value
              of said contribution

[yeah, boyee!!!
that's why the doorknob's
hittin' you . . .]

it makes me travel
        deep in self
to examine
              objectivity
of evaluation
              of self)

as monifah croons . . .

the verdict

those who know not
    the knot
of our relationship
    sit upon
the judgement chair
    listening not
to what ties the knot

as they render
their verdict
on our relationship

you be to me

bright moon
rising above shining stars
you be to me

the light
for my path in darkness
you be to me

the dawn
full of tomorrow's promises
you be to me

you be to me
the light
of my dawn's night

planting the seed

    darling
in choosing you
    i realize
our relationship
shall not consist of
        knights in shining armor
        damsels in distress
but of gardening
planting of seeds
    and nourishing them
    to maturity
        to growing old

    darling
in choosing you
    i realize
    i'm planting the seed
    of commitment

morning thoughts

in the morn when I rise
my thoughts are of you

memories of the peace found
while you slept

enshrouded in the warmth
of your sheltering bed

dreams

i dream . . .

of calling you
when i need
to hold
and be held
thru the night

i dream . . .

the wanderer

i slip on my headphones
        and let tony rich
help me leave
        the plane of this existence

to that of a traveler
        of the emotions
trying to capture
        understanding
in our actions
with each other

one destined to wander

so i listen
        to tony rich
as i leave . . .

slow slide

slowly slide
    your tongue
around my words
feeling them roll
like the gentle r

(you still hearing
mrs. thompson
from high school
french?

damn
never know where
influences come from . . .)

around my words
slowly slide

looking at you

when i look
    at you

i feel a jump
    in my right hand
        as it aches
            to touch you
and the muscles
    of restraint
        contains the urge

when i look
    at you

double dipping

the deeper the well
    the more water
        you get

that's why
    i like to
        go deep

into your

    mind

(now
    you know
        that ain't

what you really
    mean

who taught you
    about doubles?)

scorpio's ascendency

hails the coming
    of the season
    of cuddling

as arms open wide
to bring you within
their embrace

with the coming
    of the season
    of scorpio

better day

it was
    a long day
when i got home
    from the airport

heard your voice
    on the recorder

perked
    to a better day

with plans
    of future
        time

    together

all

i want to do
    is hold you

listening to your heart
    beat
  night and day

a new meaning

when you asked me
        to come meet your family
we entered a new meaning
        of us

laying in the beds
        respectfully separate
i longed to engulf you
        in my love

at the grill talking
        getting to know father
filled with warmth of you
        as he speaks

walking to the kitchen
        carrying the dishes
listening to motherly wisdom
        passed on to you

traveling the city
        with brothers and sisters
observing the display
        of love

we entered a new meaning
        of us
when you asked me . . .